Ready, Set, DINNER!

Daily Meal Planner with Recipes

@ *Journals & Notebooks*

DAY: ____

NAME: ____

	RECIPES	QTY	PROTEINS	VEGGIES	FRUITS & NUTS	FATS
Meal TIME TOTAL						

	RECIPES	QTY	PROTEINS	VEGGIES	FRUITS & NUTS	FATS
Meal TIME TOTAL						

	RECIPES	QTY	PROTEINS	VEGGIES	FRUITS & NUTS	FATS
Meal TIME TOTAL						

SNACKS TIME	

notes

DAY: ____

NAME: ____

	RECIPES	QTY	PROTEINS	VEGGIES	FRUITS & NUTS	FATS
Meal TIME TOTAL						
Meal TIME TOTAL						
Meal TIME TOTAL						
SNACKS TIME						

notes
____
____

	RECIPES	QTY	PROTEINS	VEGGIES	FRUITS & NUTS	FATS
Meal						
TIME						
TOTAL						
Meal						
TIME						
TOTAL						
Meal						
TIME						
TOTAL						
SNACKS						
TIME						

notes

DAY:

NAME:

	RECIPES	QTY	PROTEINS	VEGGIES	FRUITS & NUTS	FATS
Meal TIME						
TOTAL						
Meal TIME						
TOTAL						
Meal TIME						
TOTAL						
SNACKS TIME						

notes

DAY: ____

NAME: ____

	RECIPES	QTY	PROTEINS	VEGGIES	FRUITS & NUTS	FATS
Meal TIME						
TOTAL						
Meal TIME						
TOTAL						
Meal TIME						
TOTAL						
SNACKS TIME						

notes
____
____

DAY:

NAME:

	RECIPES	QTY	PROTEINS	VEGGIES	FRUITS & NUTS	FATS
Meal TIME TOTAL						
Meal TIME TOTAL						
Meal TIME TOTAL						
SNACKS TIME						

notes

DAY: ____

NAME: ____

	RECIPES	QTY	PROTEINS	VEGGIES	FRUITS & NUTS	FATS
Meal TIME TOTAL						
Meal TIME TOTAL						
Meal TIME TOTAL						
SNACKS TIME						

notes

DAY: ____

NAME: ____

	RECIPES	QTY	PROTEINS	VEGGIES	FRUITS & NUTS	FATS
Meal TIME						
TOTAL						
Meal TIME						
TOTAL						
Meal TIME						
TOTAL						
SNACKS TIME						

notes

DAY: ____

NAME: ____

	RECIPES	QTY	PROTEINS	VEGGIES	FRUITS & NUTS	FATS
Meal TIME						
TOTAL						
Meal TIME						
TOTAL						
Meal TIME						
TOTAL						
SNACKS TIME						

notes

DAY:

NAME:

	RECIPES	QTY	PROTEINS	VEGGIES	FRUITS & NUTS	FATS
Meal TIME						
TOTAL						
Meal TIME						
TOTAL						
Meal TIME						
TOTAL						
SNACKS TIME						

notes

DAY: ____

NAME: ____

	RECIPES	QTY	PROTEINS	VEGGIES	FRUITS & NUTS	FATS
Meal TIME ☐						
TOTAL						
Meal TIME ☐						
TOTAL						
Meal TIME ☐						
TOTAL						
SNACKS TIME ☐						

notes
____
____

DAY: ____

NAME: ____

	RECIPES	QTY	PROTEINS	VEGGIES	FRUITS & NUTS	FATS
Meal TIME [ ] TOTAL						
Meal TIME [ ] TOTAL						
Meal TIME [ ] TOTAL						
SNACKS TIME [ ]						

notes

DAY: ____

NAME: ____

	RECIPES	QTY	PROTEINS	VEGGIES	FRUITS & NUTS	FATS
Meal TIME						
TOTAL						

Meal TIME						
TOTAL						

Meal TIME						
TOTAL						

SNACKS TIME	

notes

DAY: ____

NAME: ____

	RECIPES	QTY	PROTEINS	VEGGIES	FRUITS & NUTS	FATS
Meal **TIME**						
TOTAL						
Meal **TIME**						
TOTAL						
Meal **TIME**						
TOTAL						
SNACKS **TIME**						

notes

DAY: ____

NAME: ____

	RECIPES	QTY	PROTEINS	VEGGIES	FRUITS & NUTS	FATS
Meal TIME 						
TOTAL						

	RECIPES	QTY	PROTEINS	VEGGIES	FRUITS & NUTS	FATS
Meal TIME 						
TOTAL						

	RECIPES	QTY	PROTEINS	VEGGIES	FRUITS & NUTS	FATS
Meal TIME 						
TOTAL						

SNACKS TIME 	

notes

DAY:

NAME:

	RECIPES	QTY	PROTEINS	VEGGIES	FRUITS & NUTS	FATS
Meal TIME [ ]						
TOTAL						

	RECIPES	QTY	PROTEINS	VEGGIES	FRUITS & NUTS	FATS
Meal TIME [ ]						
TOTAL						

	RECIPES	QTY	PROTEINS	VEGGIES	FRUITS & NUTS	FATS
Meal TIME [ ]						
TOTAL						

SNACKS TIME [ ]	

notes

DAY: ____

NAME: ____

	RECIPES	QTY	PROTEINS	VEGGIES	FRUITS & NUTS	FATS
Meal TIME [ ]						
TOTAL						
Meal TIME [ ]						
TOTAL						
Meal TIME [ ]						
TOTAL						
SNACKS TIME [ ]						

notes
____
____

DAY: ____

NAME: ____

	RECIPES	QTY	PROTEINS	VEGGIES	FRUITS & NUTS	FATS
Meal **TIME**						
TOTAL						

Meal **TIME**						
TOTAL						

Meal **TIME**						
TOTAL						

SNACKS **TIME**	

notes
____
____

DAY: _______________________________________

NAME: ______________________________________

	RECIPES	QTY	PROTEINS	VEGGIES	FRUITS & NUTS	FATS
Meal TIME TOTAL						

	RECIPES	QTY	PROTEINS	VEGGIES	FRUITS & NUTS	FATS
Meal TIME TOTAL						

	RECIPES	QTY	PROTEINS	VEGGIES	FRUITS & NUTS	FATS
Meal TIME TOTAL						

SNACKS TIME	

notes

DAY:

NAME:

	RECIPES	QTY	PROTEINS	VEGGIES	FRUITS & NUTS	FATS
Meal						
TIME						
TOTAL						

	RECIPES	QTY	PROTEINS	VEGGIES	FRUITS & NUTS	FATS
Meal						
TIME						
TOTAL						

	RECIPES	QTY	PROTEINS	VEGGIES	FRUITS & NUTS	FATS
Meal						
TIME						
TOTAL						

SNACKS	
TIME	

notes

DAY: ____

NAME: ____

	RECIPES	QTY	PROTEINS	VEGGIES	FRUITS & NUTS	FATS
Meal **TIME**						
TOTAL						
Meal **TIME**						
TOTAL						
Meal **TIME**						
TOTAL						
SNACKS **TIME**						

notes
____
____

DAY: ____

NAME: ____

	RECIPES	QTY	PROTEINS	VEGGIES	FRUITS & NUTS	FATS
Meal TIME 						
TOTAL						
Meal TIME 						
TOTAL						
Meal TIME 						
TOTAL						
SNACKS TIME 						

notes

DAY: ____

NAME: ____

	RECIPES	QTY	PROTEINS	VEGGIES	FRUITS & NUTS	FATS
Meal TIME TOTAL						
Meal TIME TOTAL						
Meal TIME TOTAL						
SNACKS TIME						

notes
____
____

DAY: ____

NAME: ____

	RECIPES	QTY	PROTEINS	VEGGIES	FRUITS & NUTS	FATS
Meal						
TIME						
☐						
TOTAL						
Meal						
TIME						
☐						
TOTAL						
Meal						
TIME						
☐						
TOTAL						
SNACKS						
TIME						
☐						

notes
____
____

DAY: ____

NAME: ____

	RECIPES	QTY	PROTEINS	VEGGIES	FRUITS & NUTS	FATS
Meal **TIME**						
TOTAL						
Meal **TIME**						
TOTAL						
Meal **TIME**						
TOTAL						
SNACKS **TIME**						

notes

____
____

DAY: ____

NAME: ____

	RECIPES	QTY	PROTEINS	VEGGIES	FRUITS & NUTS	FATS
Meal TIME						
TOTAL						
Meal TIME						
TOTAL						
Meal TIME						
TOTAL						
SNACKS TIME						

notes

DAY: ____

NAME: ____

	RECIPES	QTY	PROTEINS	VEGGIES	FRUITS & NUTS	FATS
Meal TIME						
TOTAL						

	RECIPES	QTY	PROTEINS	VEGGIES	FRUITS & NUTS	FATS
Meal TIME						
TOTAL						

	RECIPES	QTY	PROTEINS	VEGGIES	FRUITS & NUTS	FATS
Meal TIME						
TOTAL						

SNACKS TIME	

notes

DAY:

NAME:

	RECIPES	QTY	PROTEINS	VEGGIES	FRUITS & NUTS	FATS
Meal TIME TOTAL						
Meal TIME TOTAL						
Meal TIME TOTAL						
SNACKS TIME						

notes

DAY: ____

NAME: ____

	RECIPES	QTY	PROTEINS	VEGGIES	FRUITS & NUTS	FATS
Meal TIME						
TOTAL						

	RECIPES	QTY	PROTEINS	VEGGIES	FRUITS & NUTS	FATS
Meal TIME						
TOTAL						

	RECIPES	QTY	PROTEINS	VEGGIES	FRUITS & NUTS	FATS
Meal TIME						
TOTAL						

SNACKS TIME	

notes

DAY: ____

NAME: ____

	RECIPES	QTY	PROTEINS	VEGGIES	FRUITS & NUTS	FATS
Meal TIME TOTAL						
Meal TIME TOTAL						
Meal TIME TOTAL						
SNACKS TIME						

notes

DAY:

NAME:

	RECIPES	QTY	PROTEINS	VEGGIES	FRUITS & NUTS	FATS
Meal TIME						
TOTAL						

Meal TIME						
TOTAL						

Meal TIME						
TOTAL						

SNACKS TIME	

notes

DAY:

NAME:

	RECIPES	QTY	PROTEINS	VEGGIES	FRUITS & NUTS	FATS
Meal						
TIME						
TOTAL						
Meal						
TIME						
TOTAL						
Meal						
TIME						
TOTAL						
SNACKS						
TIME						

notes

DAY: ____

NAME: ____

	RECIPES	QTY	PROTEINS	VEGGIES	FRUITS & NUTS	FATS
Meal TIME						
TOTAL						
Meal TIME						
TOTAL						
Meal TIME						
TOTAL						
SNACKS TIME						

notes

DAY: ______________________________________

NAME: ______________________________________

	RECIPES	QTY	PROTEINS	VEGGIES	FRUITS & NUTS	FATS
Meal TIME [ ]						
TOTAL						
Meal TIME [ ]						
TOTAL						
Meal TIME [ ]						
TOTAL						
SNACKS TIME [ ]						

notes

____

____

DAY: ___________________________

NAME: ___________________________

	RECIPES	QTY	PROTEINS	VEGGIES	FRUITS & NUTS	FATS
Meal TIME						
TOTAL						

	RECIPES	QTY	PROTEINS	VEGGIES	FRUITS & NUTS	FATS
Meal TIME						
TOTAL						

	RECIPES	QTY	PROTEINS	VEGGIES	FRUITS & NUTS	FATS
Meal TIME						
TOTAL						

SNACKS TIME	

notes

DAY:

NAME:

	RECIPES	QTY	PROTEINS	VEGGIES	FRUITS & NUTS	FATS
Meal TIME						
TOTAL						
Meal TIME						
TOTAL						
Meal TIME						
TOTAL						
SNACKS TIME						

notes

DAY: ____

NAME: ____

	RECIPES	QTY	PROTEINS	VEGGIES	FRUITS & NUTS	FATS
Meal TIME						
TOTAL						
Meal TIME						
TOTAL						
Meal TIME						
TOTAL						
SNACKS TIME						

notes

DAY:

NAME:

	RECIPES	QTY	PROTEINS	VEGGIES	FRUITS & NUTS	FATS
Meal TIME						
TOTAL						
Meal TIME						
TOTAL						
Meal TIME						
TOTAL						
SNACKS TIME						

notes

DAY: ____

NAME: ____

	RECIPES	QTY	PROTEINS	VEGGIES	FRUITS & NUTS	FATS
Meal TIME [ ] TOTAL						
Meal TIME [ ] TOTAL						
Meal TIME [ ] TOTAL						
SNACKS TIME [ ]						

notes

DAY: ____

NAME: ____

	RECIPES	QTY	PROTEINS	VEGGIES	FRUITS & NUTS	FATS
Meal TIME ☐						
TOTAL						
Meal TIME ☐						
TOTAL						
Meal TIME ☐						
TOTAL						
SNACKS TIME ☐						

notes
____
____

DAY: ____

NAME: ____

	RECIPES	QTY	PROTEINS	VEGGIES	FRUITS & NUTS	FATS
Meal TIME TOTAL						
Meal TIME TOTAL						
Meal TIME TOTAL						
SNACKS TIME						

notes
____
____

DAY: ____

NAME: ____

	RECIPES	QTY	PROTEINS	VEGGIES	FRUITS & NUTS	FATS
Meal TIME TOTAL						
Meal TIME TOTAL						
Meal TIME TOTAL						
SNACKS TIME						

notes
____
____

DAY: ____

NAME: ____

	RECIPES	QTY	PROTEINS	VEGGIES	FRUITS & NUTS	FATS
Meal TIME TOTAL						
Meal TIME TOTAL						
Meal TIME TOTAL						

SNACKS TIME	

notes

DAY: ____

NAME: ____

	RECIPES	QTY	PROTEINS	VEGGIES	FRUITS & NUTS	FATS
Meal **TIME**						
TOTAL						
Meal **TIME**						
TOTAL						
Meal **TIME**						
TOTAL						
SNACKS **TIME**						

notes

____

____

DAY: ____

NAME: ____

	RECIPES	QTY	PROTEINS	VEGGIES	FRUITS & NUTS	FATS
Meal TIME TOTAL						

	RECIPES	QTY	PROTEINS	VEGGIES	FRUITS & NUTS	FATS
Meal TIME TOTAL						

	RECIPES	QTY	PROTEINS	VEGGIES	FRUITS & NUTS	FATS
Meal TIME TOTAL						

SNACKS TIME	

notes

DAY: ____

NAME: ____

	RECIPES	QTY	PROTEINS	VEGGIES	FRUITS & NUTS	FATS
Meal TIME ☐ TOTAL						
Meal TIME ☐ TOTAL						
Meal TIME ☐ TOTAL						
SNACKS TIME ☐						

notes
____
____

DAY: ____

NAME: ____

	RECIPES	QTY	PROTEINS	VEGGIES	FRUITS & NUTS	FATS
Meal						
TIME						
TOTAL						

	RECIPES	QTY	PROTEINS	VEGGIES	FRUITS & NUTS	FATS
Meal						
TIME						
TOTAL						

	RECIPES	QTY	PROTEINS	VEGGIES	FRUITS & NUTS	FATS
Meal						
TIME						
TOTAL						

SNACKS						
TIME						

notes

DAY:

NAME:

	RECIPES	QTY	PROTEINS	VEGGIES	FRUITS & NUTS	FATS
Meal TIME						
TOTAL						

	RECIPES	QTY	PROTEINS	VEGGIES	FRUITS & NUTS	FATS
Meal TIME						
TOTAL						

	RECIPES	QTY	PROTEINS	VEGGIES	FRUITS & NUTS	FATS
Meal TIME						
TOTAL						

SNACKS TIME	

notes

DAY: _______________________________________

NAME: _______________________________________

	RECIPES	QTY	PROTEINS	VEGGIES	FRUITS & NUTS	FATS
Meal TIME						
TOTAL						
Meal TIME						
TOTAL						
Meal TIME						
TOTAL						
SNACKS TIME						

notes

____

____

DAY:

NAME:

	RECIPES	QTY	PROTEINS	VEGGIES	FRUITS & NUTS	FATS
Meal TIME						
TOTAL						
Meal TIME						
TOTAL						
Meal TIME						
TOTAL						
SNACKS TIME						

notes

DAY: ____

NAME: ____

	RECIPES	QTY	PROTEINS	VEGGIES	FRUITS & NUTS	FATS
Meal TIME						
TOTAL						
Meal TIME						
TOTAL						
Meal TIME						
TOTAL						
SNACKS TIME						

notes
____
____

DAY: ____

NAME: ____

	RECIPES	QTY	PROTEINS	VEGGIES	FRUITS & NUTS	FATS
Meal TIME						
TOTAL						
Meal TIME						
TOTAL						
Meal TIME						
TOTAL						
SNACKS TIME						

notes
____
____

DAY: ____

NAME: ____

	RECIPES	QTY	PROTEINS	VEGGIES	FRUITS & NUTS	FATS
Meal **TIME** [ ] **TOTAL**						
Meal **TIME** [ ] **TOTAL**						
Meal **TIME** [ ] **TOTAL**						
SNACKS **TIME** [ ]						

notes

____

____

DAY:

NAME:

	RECIPES	QTY	PROTEINS	VEGGIES	FRUITS & NUTS	FATS
Meal TIME						
TOTAL						
Meal TIME						
TOTAL						
Meal TIME						
TOTAL						
SNACKS TIME						

notes

DAY: _______________________________________

NAME: ______________________________________

	RECIPES	QTY	PROTEINS	VEGGIES	FRUITS & NUTS	FATS
Meal **TIME**						
TOTAL						
Meal **TIME**						
TOTAL						
Meal **TIME**						
TOTAL						
SNACKS **TIME**						

notes

DAY:

NAME:

	RECIPES	QTY	PROTEINS	VEGGIES	FRUITS & NUTS	FATS
Meal TIME						
TOTAL						
Meal TIME						
TOTAL						
Meal TIME						
TOTAL						
SNACKS TIME						

notes

DAY: ____

NAME: ____

	RECIPES	QTY	PROTEINS	VEGGIES	FRUITS & NUTS	FATS
Meal **TIME**						
TOTAL						
Meal **TIME**						
TOTAL						
Meal **TIME**						
TOTAL						
SNACKS **TIME**						

notes

____

DAY: ____

NAME: ____

	RECIPES	QTY	PROTEINS	VEGGIES	FRUITS & NUTS	FATS
Meal TIME						
TOTAL						
Meal TIME						
TOTAL						
Meal TIME						
TOTAL						
SNACKS TIME						

notes

DAY: ____

NAME: ____

	RECIPES	QTY	PROTEINS	VEGGIES	FRUITS & NUTS	FATS
Meal TIME						
TOTAL						
Meal TIME						
TOTAL						
Meal TIME						
TOTAL						
SNACKS TIME						

notes

DAY:

NAME:

	RECIPES	QTY	PROTEINS	VEGGIES	FRUITS & NUTS	FATS
Meal						
TIME						
TOTAL						
Meal						
TIME						
TOTAL						
Meal						
TIME						
TOTAL						
SNACKS						
TIME						

notes

DAY: ____

NAME: ____

	RECIPES	QTY	PROTEINS	VEGGIES	FRUITS & NUTS	FATS
Meal TIME TOTAL						
Meal TIME TOTAL						
Meal TIME TOTAL						
SNACKS TIME						

notes

DAY:

NAME:

	RECIPES	QTY	PROTEINS	VEGGIES	FRUITS & NUTS	FATS
Meal TIME TOTAL						
Meal TIME TOTAL						
Meal TIME TOTAL						
SNACKS TIME						

notes

DAY: ______________________________

NAME: ______________________________

	RECIPES	QTY	PROTEINS	VEGGIES	FRUITS & NUTS	FATS
Meal TIME						
TOTAL						

Meal TIME					
TOTAL					

Meal TIME					
TOTAL					

SNACKS TIME	

notes
____
____

DAY: ____

NAME: ____

	RECIPES	QTY	PROTEINS	VEGGIES	FRUITS & NUTS	FATS
Meal TIME [ ]						
TOTAL						
Meal TIME [ ]						
TOTAL						
Meal TIME [ ]						
TOTAL						
SNACKS TIME [ ]						

notes

____

DAY: ____

NAME: ____

	RECIPES	QTY	PROTEINS	VEGGIES	FRUITS & NUTS	FATS
Meal TIME						
TOTAL						
Meal TIME						
TOTAL						
Meal TIME						
TOTAL						
SNACKS TIME						

notes
____
____

DAY: ____

NAME: ____

	RECIPES	QTY	PROTEINS	VEGGIES	FRUITS & NUTS	FATS
Meal TIME						
TOTAL						
Meal TIME						
TOTAL						
Meal TIME						
TOTAL						
SNACKS TIME						

notes

DAY: _______________________________

NAME: _______________________________

	RECIPES	QTY	PROTEINS	VEGGIES	FRUITS & NUTS	FATS
Meal TIME						
TOTAL						
Meal TIME						
TOTAL						
Meal TIME						
TOTAL						
SNACKS TIME						

notes

	RECIPES	QTY	PROTEINS	VEGGIES	FRUITS & NUTS	FATS
Meal						
TIME						
TOTAL						
Meal						
TIME						
TOTAL						
Meal						
TIME						
TOTAL						
SNACKS						
TIME						

notes

DAY:

NAME:

	RECIPES	QTY	PROTEINS	VEGGIES	FRUITS & NUTS	FATS
Meal TIME						
TOTAL						

	RECIPES	QTY	PROTEINS	VEGGIES	FRUITS & NUTS	FATS
Meal TIME						
TOTAL						

	RECIPES	QTY	PROTEINS	VEGGIES	FRUITS & NUTS	FATS
Meal TIME						
TOTAL						

SNACKS TIME	

notes

DAY: ____

NAME: ____

	RECIPES	QTY	PROTEINS	VEGGIES	FRUITS & NUTS	FATS
Meal						
TIME						
TOTAL						

	RECIPES	QTY	PROTEINS	VEGGIES	FRUITS & NUTS	FATS
Meal						
TIME						
TOTAL						

	RECIPES	QTY	PROTEINS	VEGGIES	FRUITS & NUTS	FATS
Meal						
TIME						
TOTAL						

SNACKS	
TIME	

notes
____
____

DAY: ____

NAME: ____

	RECIPES	QTY	PROTEINS	VEGGIES	FRUITS & NUTS	FATS
Meal TIME [ ]						
TOTAL						
Meal TIME [ ]						
TOTAL						
Meal TIME [ ]						
TOTAL						
SNACKS TIME [ ]						

notes
____
____

DAY:
NAME:

	RECIPES	QTY	PROTEINS	VEGGIES	FRUITS & NUTS	FATS
Meal TIME						
TOTAL						
Meal TIME						
TOTAL						
Meal TIME						
TOTAL						
SNACKS TIME						

notes

DAY:

NAME:

	RECIPES	QTY	PROTEINS	VEGGIES	FRUITS & NUTS	FATS
Meal TIME TOTAL						
Meal TIME TOTAL						
Meal TIME TOTAL						
SNACKS TIME						

notes

DAY:

NAME:

	RECIPES	QTY	PROTEINS	VEGGIES	FRUITS & NUTS	FATS
Meal TIME						
TOTAL						
Meal TIME						
TOTAL						
Meal TIME						
TOTAL						
SNACKS TIME						

notes

DAY: ____

NAME: ____

	RECIPES	QTY	PROTEINS	VEGGIES	FRUITS & NUTS	FATS
Meal TIME TOTAL						
Meal TIME TOTAL						
Meal TIME TOTAL						
SNACKS TIME						

notes
____
____

DAY:

NAME:

	RECIPES	QTY	PROTEINS	VEGGIES	FRUITS & NUTS	FATS
Meal TIME						
TOTAL						
Meal TIME						
TOTAL						
Meal TIME						
TOTAL						
SNACKS TIME						

notes

DAY: ____

NAME: ____

	RECIPES	QTY	PROTEINS	VEGGIES	FRUITS & NUTS	FATS
Meal TIME						
TOTAL						

	RECIPES	QTY	PROTEINS	VEGGIES	FRUITS & NUTS	FATS
Meal TIME						
TOTAL						

	RECIPES	QTY	PROTEINS	VEGGIES	FRUITS & NUTS	FATS
Meal TIME						
TOTAL						

SNACKS TIME	

notes

DAY:

NAME:

	RECIPES	QTY	PROTEINS	VEGGIES	FRUITS & NUTS	FATS
Meal TIME						
TOTAL						
Meal TIME						
TOTAL						
Meal TIME						
TOTAL						
SNACKS TIME						

notes

DAY: ____

NAME: ____

	RECIPES	QTY	PROTEINS	VEGGIES	FRUITS & NUTS	FATS
Meal TIME						
TOTAL						
Meal TIME						
TOTAL						
Meal TIME						
TOTAL						
SNACKS TIME						

notes

DAY: _______________________________________

NAME: _______________________________________

	RECIPES	QTY	PROTEINS	VEGGIES	FRUITS & NUTS	FATS
Meal **TIME** 						
TOTAL						
Meal **TIME** 						
TOTAL						
Meal **TIME** 						
TOTAL						
SNACKS **TIME** 						

notes

DAY: ____

NAME: ____

	RECIPES	QTY	PROTEINS	VEGGIES	FRUITS & NUTS	FATS
Meal TIME						
TOTAL						

	RECIPES	QTY	PROTEINS	VEGGIES	FRUITS & NUTS	FATS
Meal TIME						
TOTAL						

	RECIPES	QTY	PROTEINS	VEGGIES	FRUITS & NUTS	FATS
Meal TIME						
TOTAL						

SNACKS TIME	

notes

DAY: ____

NAME: ____

	RECIPES	QTY	PROTEINS	VEGGIES	FRUITS & NUTS	FATS
Meal TIME						
TOTAL						
Meal TIME						
TOTAL						
Meal TIME						
TOTAL						
SNACKS TIME						

notes

DAY: ____

NAME: ____

	RECIPES	QTY	PROTEINS	VEGGIES	FRUITS & NUTS	FATS
Meal **TIME**						
TOTAL						
Meal **TIME**						
TOTAL						
Meal **TIME**						
TOTAL						
SNACKS **TIME**						

notes

____

____

DAY: ____

NAME: ____

	RECIPES	QTY	PROTEINS	VEGGIES	FRUITS & NUTS	FATS
Meal TIME ⬚						
TOTAL						

	RECIPES	QTY	PROTEINS	VEGGIES	FRUITS & NUTS	FATS
Meal TIME ⬚						
TOTAL						

	RECIPES	QTY	PROTEINS	VEGGIES	FRUITS & NUTS	FATS
Meal TIME ⬚						
TOTAL						

SNACKS TIME ⬚	

notes

DAY: ____

NAME: ____

	RECIPES	QTY	PROTEINS	VEGGIES	FRUITS & NUTS	FATS
Meal TIME						
TOTAL						
Meal TIME						
TOTAL						
Meal TIME						
TOTAL						
SNACKS TIME						

notes

DAY: ____

NAME: ____

	RECIPES	QTY	PROTEINS	VEGGIES	FRUITS & NUTS	FATS
Meal						
TIME						
TOTAL						

	RECIPES	QTY	PROTEINS	VEGGIES	FRUITS & NUTS	FATS
Meal						
TIME						
TOTAL						

	RECIPES	QTY	PROTEINS	VEGGIES	FRUITS & NUTS	FATS
Meal						
TIME						
TOTAL						

SNACKS	
TIME	

notes

DAY: _______________________________________

NAME: _______________________________________

	RECIPES	QTY	PROTEINS	VEGGIES	FRUITS & NUTS	FATS
Meal TIME TOTAL						
Meal TIME TOTAL						
Meal TIME TOTAL						
SNACKS TIME						

notes

DAY: ____

NAME: ____

	RECIPES	QTY	PROTEINS	VEGGIES	FRUITS & NUTS	FATS
Meal TIME TOTAL						
Meal TIME TOTAL						
Meal TIME TOTAL						
SNACKS TIME						

notes
____
____

DAY: ____

NAME: ____

	RECIPES	QTY	PROTEINS	VEGGIES	FRUITS & NUTS	FATS
Meal TIME						
TOTAL						

	RECIPES	QTY	PROTEINS	VEGGIES	FRUITS & NUTS	FATS
Meal TIME						
TOTAL						

	RECIPES	QTY	PROTEINS	VEGGIES	FRUITS & NUTS	FATS
Meal TIME						
TOTAL						

SNACKS TIME	

notes
____
____

DAY: ____

NAME: ____

	RECIPES	QTY	PROTEINS	VEGGIES	FRUITS & NUTS	FATS
Meal **TIME**						
TOTAL						
Meal **TIME**						
TOTAL						
Meal **TIME**						
TOTAL						
SNACKS **TIME**						

notes
____
____

DAY: ____

NAME: ____

	RECIPES	QTY	PROTEINS	VEGGIES	FRUITS & NUTS	FATS
Meal TIME [ ]						
TOTAL						
Meal TIME [ ]						
TOTAL						
Meal TIME [ ]						
TOTAL						
SNACKS TIME [ ]						

notes
____
____

DAY:

NAME:

	RECIPES	QTY	PROTEINS	VEGGIES	FRUITS & NUTS	FATS
Meal TIME						
TOTAL						

Meal TIME						
TOTAL						

Meal TIME						
TOTAL						

SNACKS TIME	

notes

DAY:

NAME:

	RECIPES	QTY	PROTEINS	VEGGIES	FRUITS & NUTS	FATS
Meal TIME TOTAL						
Meal TIME TOTAL						
Meal TIME TOTAL						
SNACKS TIME						

notes

DAY:

NAME:

	RECIPES	QTY	PROTEINS	VEGGIES	FRUITS & NUTS	FATS
Meal TIME TOTAL						

	RECIPES	QTY	PROTEINS	VEGGIES	FRUITS & NUTS	FATS
Meal TIME TOTAL						

	RECIPES	QTY	PROTEINS	VEGGIES	FRUITS & NUTS	FATS
Meal TIME TOTAL						

SNACKS TIME	

notes

DAY: ____

NAME: ____

	RECIPES	QTY	PROTEINS	VEGGIES	FRUITS & NUTS	FATS
Meal TIME						
TOTAL						
Meal TIME						
TOTAL						
Meal TIME						
TOTAL						
SNACKS TIME						

notes

DAY: _______________________________________

NAME: _______________________________________

	RECIPES	QTY	PROTEINS	VEGGIES	FRUITS & NUTS	FATS
Meal TIME [ ]						
TOTAL						
Meal TIME [ ]						
TOTAL						
Meal TIME [ ]						
TOTAL						
SNACKS TIME [ ]						

notes

____

____

DAY:

NAME:

	RECIPES	QTY	PROTEINS	VEGGIES	FRUITS & NUTS	FATS
Meal TIME						
TOTAL						
Meal TIME						
TOTAL						
Meal TIME						
TOTAL						
SNACKS TIME						

notes

DAY: ____

NAME: ____

	RECIPES	QTY	PROTEINS	VEGGIES	FRUITS & NUTS	FATS
Meal TIME TOTAL						
Meal TIME TOTAL						
Meal TIME TOTAL						
SNACKS TIME						

notes

DAY:

NAME:

	RECIPES	QTY	PROTEINS	VEGGIES	FRUITS & NUTS	FATS
Meal TIME TOTAL						
Meal TIME TOTAL						
Meal TIME TOTAL						
SNACKS TIME						

notes

DAY:

NAME:

	RECIPES	QTY	PROTEINS	VEGGIES	FRUITS & NUTS	FATS
Meal TIME						
TOTAL						
Meal TIME						
TOTAL						
Meal TIME						
TOTAL						
SNACKS TIME						

notes

DAY: _______________________________

NAME: _______________________________

	RECIPES	QTY	PROTEINS	VEGGIES	FRUITS & NUTS	FATS
Meal TIME TOTAL						
Meal TIME TOTAL						
Meal TIME TOTAL						
SNACKS TIME						

notes

DAY:

NAME:

	RECIPES	QTY	PROTEINS	VEGGIES	FRUITS & NUTS	FATS
Meal TIME						
TOTAL						
Meal TIME						
TOTAL						
Meal TIME						
TOTAL						
SNACKS TIME						

notes

DAY: ____

NAME: ____

	RECIPES	QTY	PROTEINS	VEGGIES	FRUITS & NUTS	FATS
Meal TIME TOTAL						
Meal TIME TOTAL						
Meal TIME TOTAL						
SNACKS TIME						

notes
____
____

DAY: ____

NAME: ____

	RECIPES	QTY	PROTEINS	VEGGIES	FRUITS & NUTS	FATS
Meal TIME						
TOTAL						

	RECIPES	QTY	PROTEINS	VEGGIES	FRUITS & NUTS	FATS
Meal TIME						
TOTAL						

	RECIPES	QTY	PROTEINS	VEGGIES	FRUITS & NUTS	FATS
Meal TIME						
TOTAL						

SNACKS TIME	

notes
____
____